PRAYING AS
Jesus
TAUGHT US

✳

Meditations on the
OUR FATHER

. . .

PRAYING AS
Jesus
TAUGHT US

✴

Meditations on the
OUR FATHER

. . .

CARDINAL
CARLO MARIA MARTINI

Translated by JOHN BELMONTE, S.J.

SHEED & WARD
Franklin, Wisconsin

As an apostolate of the Priests of the Sacred Heart, a Catholic religious congregation, the mission of Sheed & Ward is to publish books of contemporary impact and enduring merit in Catholic Christian thought and action. The books published, however, reflect the opinion of their authors and are not meant to represent the official position of the Priests of the Sacred Heart.

2001

Sheed & Ward
7373 South Lovers Lane Road
Franklin, Wisconsin 53132
1-800-266-5564

Originally published and © in 1999 by In Dialogo Cooperativa Culturale srl., Via S. Antonio, 5 – 20122 Milano

Printed in the United States of America.

Cover and interior design: Robin Costa Booth
Cover art: Copyright © 2000 by the Passionist Research Center. "Jesus Teaches Children." Stained glass window at St. Mary's Church in McKees Rocks, Pennsylvania. Photograph taken by Fr. John Render, C.P., D. Min. Used with permission.

Library of Congress Cataloging-in-Publication Data

Martini, Carlo Maria, 1927–
    [Padre nostro. English]
    Praying as Jesus taught us : meditations on the Our Father / Carlo Maria Martini ; translated by John Belmonte.
        p. cm.
    ISBN 1-58051-087-6 (alk. paper)
        1. Lord's Prayer—Meditations. I. Title.

BV230 .M37 2001
226.9'606—dc21

00-053813

1 2 3 4 5 / 04 03 02 01

CONTENTS

TRANSLATOR'S
INTRODUCTION

This book is for seekers and pilgrims. It offers a simple yet significant way to come to the beginning and end of all our journeys, an encounter with Jesus Christ. As part of the Church's preparation for the Jubilee Year, Pope John Paul II suggested reflecting on the "Father who is in heaven." Cardinal Carlo Maria Martini, Archbishop of Milan and an internationally known biblical scholar and writer on the spiritual life, took that suggestion seriously.

During Lent 1999 Cardinal Martini led his diocese through a series of catechetical lessons based on the Our Father. Broadcast by television and radio, these five meditations took place at five different locations in Milan, each location dramatically emphasizing one aspect of the prayer Jesus taught his disciples. The pilgrimage began at the archbishop's palace, or Arcivescovado, in order to connect the diocese in prayer with the saintly bishops who preceded Martini, among whom include Cardinal Montini, later Pope Paul VI. The pilgrimage then went to Luigi Sacco Hospital to focus attention on human suffering and our need to be delivered from evil. The third stop on the pilgrimage was the Prison of San Vittore, which served to dramatically highlight our need for forgiveness, freedom, and reconciliation. The pilgrims then visited the Monastery of the Poor Clares, a place of contemplative prayer that emphasized the importance of doing God's will. Finally, the Lenten journey of the diocese concluded at the parish of St. Mary Beltrade, an ordinary parish that provided a fitting place to conclude, since parish life is the ordinary place where we seek the sanctification offered to us through the Church.

The result of Cardinal Martini's pilgrimage is this collection of meditations that you hold in your hands. By exploring the most familiar words in all of Scripture — the Our Father — you become a pilgrim sent out by the Pope, accompanied by a cardinal, and guided by Jesus' prayer. What better way to come to know Jesus and how he understood himself, his vocation, and his mission, and to answer his invitation to journey with him!

Like any journey, the expected and the unexpected are possible. The prayer on which you will meditate is perhaps the first you ever learned. You know what to expect. You know every word by heart and can find in that familiarity a deep consolation. However, Cardinal Martini, our wise and experienced guide, also offers us the unexpected. He has altered the order of the petitions, emphasizing first what he calls the most universal human experiences: evil, temptation, hunger. Later, he passes on to the most important petitions, those that have to do with God.

The effect is typical of the newness of the spiritual life. The prayer so familiar to us that we can recite it without thought, we hear now as if for the first time. Saint Paul mentions something similar in his first letter to the church at Corinth: through the Spirit, God reveals to us who love him, "what no eye has seen, nor ear heard" (2:9). For the spiritual pilgrimage of each one of us, both the expected and the unexpected parts, our point of departure is our place of return: the Father of all through our encounter with Jesus Christ in the Spirit.

JOHN BELMONTE, S.J.

INTRODUCTION

BY CARDINAL CARLO MARIA MARTINI

The itinerary of the Lenten catechesis begins this year in the chapel of the Arcivescovado, a very important, historic place. It was built around 1570 and has welcomed, over the centuries, the prayer of many holy bishops: from Charles Borromeo to Andrea Carlo Ferrari, from Idlefonso Schuster to Giovanni Battista Montini, later Pope Paul VI.

We can then ask for their intercession over the course of our reflections, especially since the selected theme is truly arduous. The Pope suggested it in his apostolic letter, *Tertio millenio adveniente:*

1999, the third and final preparatory year of the Great Jubilee will be aimed at broadening the horizons of believers, so that they will see things in the perspective of Christ: in the perspective of the "Father who is in heaven" (cf. Mt. 5:45), from whom the Lord was sent and to whom he has returned (n. 49).

For this reason we want to contemplate the mystery of the Father by meditating on the prayer of the Our Father.

By way of introduction, let us listen to two gospel texts:

"When you are praying, do not heap up empty phrases as the Gentiles do; for they think that they will be heard because of their many words. Do not be like them, for your Father knows what you need before you ask him.

"Pray then in this way:

"Our Father in heaven,
    hallowed be your name"
    (Matthew 6:9).

They went to a place called Geth-
semane; and he said to his disciples,
"Sit here while I pray." He took with
him Peter, James, and John, and began
to be distressed and agitated. And said
to them, "I am deeply grieved, even to
death; remain here and keep awake."
And going a little farther, he threw himself on the ground and prayed that, if it
were possible, the hour might pass by
him. He said, "Abba, Father, for you all
things are possible; remove this cup
from me; yet not what I want, but what
you want" (Mark 14:32–36).

I confess to experiencing a bit of trepidation
before the prayer that Jesus taught us, because it
surpasses us in every way and, in order to
understand it, we will have to penetrate deeply
into the riches of Jesus' own feelings, into his
heart. Besides that, I maintain that it is objec-
tively difficult to speak of the Our Father in an
abstract way. Being a prayer, one understands it
by praying it. What I will seek to express is
simply a function of your personal prayer.

THE PRAYER OF THE OUR FATHER

Before considering the invocations of the Our Father, I want to make three observations.

First of all, it is a very simple and brief prayer. We know others that are longer, also in the New Testament. There are others which seem to be more rich in affect, as for example that prayer of Charles de Foucauld, which begins like this, "Father of mine, I abandon myself to you, make of me that which is pleasing to you. Whatever you might do to me, I thank you." Instead, the Our Father reminds us of the pillars of a great cathedral, rigid pillars but ones which support an immense building.

Also it is a prayer that is apparently a bit generic. It has been said — I believe correctly — that it could be recited by followers of every religion. All of those who refer themselves to God could repeat the words of the Our Father.

On the other hand, it is a synthetic prayer, one that summarizes the entire gospel — and one understands fully the single invocations only by reading them in the light of the gospel. However, paradoxically, the Our Father can be recited by every man and woman of goodwill, whatever might be the religion to which they belong. Nevertheless, it reveals its secret in the measure in which it is understood in the light of the gospel. It is a synthesis of the whole life of Jesus and the key to understanding his entire life.

Our Father

AT THE ARCIVESCOVADO,
THE ARCHBISHOP'S PALACE

O God our Father,

this is how we learned to call you;

this is how your son Jesus taught us!

Help us to understand

the immensity of this revelation

and turn ourselves in trust to you

in the moments of joy

and in those of pain,

when we are rich in hope

and when sadness is victorious,

because you alone know how to sustain

us along life's journey.

Through Christ our Lord.

Amen.

"Our Father who art in heaven"

That a biblical prayer should begin with the exclamation "Father" is out of the ordinary. For example, the Psalms, which are 150 beautiful prayers, never begin with that exclamation. It is uniquely characteristic, then, of the way Jesus prayed and how he wanted to communicate with us.

I would like to explain what "Father" meant in Jesus' experience, in the experience of his disciples, and in the experience of individual Christians.

"FATHER" IN JESUS' EXPERIENCE

From the Gospels we know that when Jesus mentions God he almost always calls him by the name "Father." Indeed, for the Evangelist Luke, the first spoken words of Jesus have to do with the Father; it is the famous episode of the twelve-year-old Jesus who, found by his parents in the Jerusalem Temple, says, "Did you not know that I must be in my Father's house?" (Luke 2:49). He will continue in like manner until the end of his life, even unto the supreme test, as the Markan text which I mentioned in the introduction suggests to us: "Abba, Father, for you all things are possible." And again, on the cross, while he is about to die: "Father, forgive them; for they do not know what they are doing . . . Father, into your hands I commend my spirit" (Luke 23:34, 46).

The name Father is consequently and first of all used by Jesus, in the form that, in the Aramaic language of the time, indicated the familiar address with which young children would call their fathers: "Abba." It is a most tender name, one that evokes a world of affection, trust, and surrender. It is an appellation that qualifies the experience of Jesus. He lives

6

his sonship and teaches us to call God using the same word that he uses. It is neither a word that we could invent nor is it by chance that it is placed before us in the liturgy at the recitation or singing of the Our Father, with the verb, "We dare to say." We would not have dared to pronounce the name Father if Jesus had not given it to us.

Precisely because this invocation is not only placed on our lips but also introduces to us Jesus' way of praying, it is rather difficult to explain. I highlighted this aspect in my pastoral letter, "Return to the Father of All": "The perception that the Christian has of the mystery of the Father is inexpressible in words, but is grounded in the perception that Jesus Christ the Son has of it, and it is entrusted to the grace of the Holy Spirit. This mystery of the Father goes beyond, therefore, any thought or concept, it is not bound by mere words, it is always 'beyond.' Even so, much has been given us to grasp part of it through Jesus' word, '*Abba*'"(n. 5. p. 33). And we learn from the intensity with which Jesus expressed the word *Abba*.

In the Matthean text, the exclamation "Our Father" is followed by the addition "who art in heaven." With pleasure, let us pause awhile on this expression, because it is particularly important. It has the purpose of not only distinguishing the divine and universal paternity from every human paternity, but it also serves to indicate heaven as the place of definitive realities, where the paternity of God reveals itself in its fullness. It is the place from which the Kingdom that comes to us in Matthew's Gospel is called "the Kingdom of heaven"; the Kingdom that is with the Father and from there comes to earth.

The expression "who art in heaven" — other than suggesting to us the symbolic gesture of casting our gaze heavenward like Jesus who, when praying, would raise his eyes to heaven — comes to us from the destination of our journey, from the place of definitive goods, and communicates to us the inexhaustible experience of Jesus himself, an experience that we will contemplate for all of eternity.

"FATHER" IN THE DISCIPLES' EXPERIENCE

Let us seek now to understand what the expression "Our Father who art in heaven" meant in the experience of the first disciples. They left everything to follow Jesus. And although they were with Jesus, they weren't any more secure in their bread, housing, or the welcome they would receive. In fact, they faced persecution and rejection.

Prayerful invocation to the Father for them meant an act of intense trust: this Father knows everything about us, knows our precarious, fragile condition, and certainly will provide for us. That passage from Matthew that we heard at the beginning comes to mind here: "Your Father knows what you need before you ask him." Another saying of Jesus fits here: "Do not be afraid, little flock, for it is your Father's good pleasure to give you the kingdom" (Luke 12:32). You are small and few but the Father gives you the Kingdom.

When we repeat the exclamation, "Our Father who art in heaven," we enter into either the feelings and thoughts of Jesus or the experience of the first disciples, who felt themselves grow in reliance on the Father.

"FATHER" IN CHRISTIANS' EXPERIENCE

Let us consider, finally, the expression "Our Father who art in heaven" in our own experience, in the experience of every Christian.

First of all, it is not human experience but it is given to us by the Holy Spirit. The apostle Paul forcefully reminds us of this: "You have received a spirit of adoption. When we cry, 'Abba! Father!' it is that very Spirit bearing witness with our spirit that we are children of God" (Romans 8:15–16); "And because you are children, God has sent the Spirit of his Son into our hearts, crying, 'Abba! Father!'" (Galatians 4:6).

So the words of the Our Father are correlated with the experience of the children of God. Every time we pronounce the name "Father," I hear the appellation, "child, my child, my children." My invocation is answered by the sense of God's progeny whereby God claims me—indeed, each one of us.

We can then intuit the feelings the name "Father" stirs up in us when we say it with intensity. First, the feeling of being profoundly understood: God knows that for which I have the greatest need. Next, the feeling of being important in God's eyes, as in the moment in which the prodigal son in the parable was embraced by the father. If God permits us to call him Father, it means that we are of great value to him. From this also comes the feeling of not being abandoned during times of trial, but of being understood, supported, accompanied. And finally, there is the feeling of being able to turn to God with conviction. If he is Father, we are free to speak to him with frankness.

The appellation "Father" is so important that, ideally, it is placed before every invocation of prayer: Father, your Kingdom come; Father, thy will be done; Father, give us our bread; Father, forgive us our trespasses.

We ask ourselves: To what kind of sentimentality does this appellation stand in opposition? It stands in opposition to pretentious prayer that presumes fulfillment by the simple power of words. It stands in opposition to prayer recited without conviction, distrustful prayer that drags itself along in a monotonous and arid way. Quite to the contrary, the Our Father generates surrender, drives out any pretense, and sustains our reliance on God.

"Hallowed be thy name"

Continuing the explanation, I want to pause very briefly on the expression "hallowed be thy name." It is rather strange and is not part of our everyday language. In order to understand it we must return to a page from the prophet Ezekiel:

> Therefore say to the house of Israel, Thus says the Lord GOD: It is not for your sake, O house of Israel, that I am about to act, but for the sake of my holy name, which you have profaned among the nations to which you came. I will sanctify my great name, which has been profaned among the nations, and which you have profaned among them; and the nations shall know that I am the LORD, says the Lord GOD, when through you I display my holiness before their eyes. I will take you from the nations, and gather you from all the countries, and bring you into your own land. I will sprinkle clean water upon you, and you shall be clean from

all your uncleannesses, and from all
your idols I will cleanse you. A new
heart I will give you, and a new spirit
I will put within you; and I will
remove from your body the heart of
stone and give you a heart of flesh
(Ezekiel 36:22–26).

This text is the key to the invocation "hallowed be thy name" because it introduces the
contrary expression as well. In fact, to paraphrase, the Lord says to his people: "You have
profaned my name. In as much as your depor-
tation, caused by your sins, has appeared as
the defeat of God, it made our enemies think
that my name isn't worth anything. But I,
instead, will prove the holiness of my great
name, I will show how much I am worth and I
will liberate you."

In light of the prophecy of Ezekiel, we can
paraphrase the invocation of the Our Father
like this: "Prove the holiness of your name, O
Father, make known that you are good, that you
are strong, that you love us!" It is a way of pro-
voking God to reveal his love for us and his

power, in line with the conviction about which I spoke before.

Questions for Personal Reflection

In the desire to illuminate the very first words of the prayer Jesus taught us, I opened a window on the world of thoughts, ideas, doctrine, that we will gradually penetrate. At this point, however, I propose three questions for your reflection, recovering them from my pastoral letter "Return to the Father of All."

1. What image do I have of God the Father? Is it the God of Jesus? Do I trust myself unfailingly to him, placing in his hands all my anguish and fears?

2. (The second question touches us primarily as catechists and educators.) What face of God is communicated by my catechesis and in my preaching? Is it the Father of Jesus?

3. (The proof of whether or not you know God as Father, your Father and Father of all, can be verified in a number of ways.)

Do I feel like thanking God for everything that happens to me? Am I able to overcome the anguish or trouble of things that hang over me without those things causing me to lose contact with real situations? Am I capable of putting up with an injustice without continual recriminations in my heart, justifying myself and defending myself? Am I able to say, "I trust in the steadfast love of God forever and ever" (Psalm 52:8)?

These questions will allow us to understand if the words of the Our Father have truly penetrated us and have produced as fruit the attitude of peace, of trust, of reliance, that Jesus lived speaking of the Father and entrusting himself to him.

❋ II ❋

Deliver Us from Evil

AT LUIGI SACCO HOSPITAL

O God, you know

our fragility and our weaknesses,

sustain us in the trials

that life presents us.

We know that,

sustained by your help,

we can defeat evil.

Make us always perceive

your nearness and your support,

so that we feel neither alone nor defeated,

but ready to walk in hope.

Through Christ our Lord.

Amen.

*T*he prayer of the Our Father is situated this evening in a place that accepts suffering, that works through health to liberate from evil. We find ourselves, in fact, in the chapel of a hospital, and we want to deepen together our understanding of the invocation taught to us by Jesus, "Father, deliver us from evil."

Two texts from the New Testament will guide us in our reflection.

I am writing to you, fathers,
because you know him who is

from the beginning.
I am writing to you, young people,
   because you have conquered
   the evil one.
I write to you, children,
   because you know the Father.
I write to you, fathers,
   because you know him who is
   from the beginning.
I write to you, young people,
   because you are strong
   and the word of God abides in you,
   and you have overcome the evil one.
   (1 John 2:13–14).

Finally, brothers and sisters, pray for us, so that the word of the Lord may spread rapidly and be glorified everywhere, just as it is among you, and that we may be rescued from wicked and evil people; for not all have faith. But the Lord is faithful; he will strengthen you and guard you from the evil one (2 Thessalonians 3:1–3).

By way of introduction, I would like to cite some words of commentary on the Our Father from Simone Weil, a great religious thinker of Jewish origin, who died very young in 1943. She says: "This prayer contains in it all possible riches. It is impossible to say it just once concentrating one's own attention on every word without some real change, be it even infinitesimal, being produced in the soul" (S. Weil, *Attesa di Dio*, Milano, 1972, p. 194). We intend to concentrate on one word of this most beautiful of prayers in the desire that a change might occur in our soul: growth in hope and trust. We can be astonished that the Our Father, which begins with an affectionate naming, concludes with the term *evil*. Simone Weil explains it like this: "With the word 'Father' the prayer has its beginning, with the word 'evil' it has its conclusion. One must pass from trust to fear, only trust gives sufficient strength so that fear does not cause downfall or failure" (S. Weil, p. 192).

The Sapiential Order
of the Invocations

In our first meeting we sought to penetrate the meaning of the invocation, "Our Father, who art in heaven, hallowed be thy name." I prefer this evening not to follow the order that would lead us to dwell on the invocation "thy will be done" for one simple reason. "Deliver us from evil" is the first cry of the heart of the one who feels assailed by every form of evil. It is the most elemental petition, the most simple supplication. It is the prayer proper to those who are sick, who want their suffering lifted immediately, and it is a universal prayer.

There is, therefore, an order in the petitions of the Our Father that we can call *sapiential* or *wisdom*, that is, one of values. It begins from the most important realities, those that have to do with God—like the sanctification of the Name, the coming of the Kingdom, the fulfillment of the divine will—and it moves toward the realities which are closer to us, like bread, debts, temptation, evil.

Beyond this order of values, there is another order, one which is more *pedagogical*, didactic, that I chose to follow specifically: to begin from that of which we have the greatest experience, like of evil, temptation, sins, hunger. These are petitions that we can find on the lips of believers and nonbelievers, of the followers of every religion, because there is no experience more universal than that of evil.

And, in the Our Father, the invocation "deliver us" or "tear us away from" evil parallels the invocation immediately preceding, "do not permit that we are overcome by temptation," indicating how the power of evil lurks behind every temptation and pervades the world.

"Deliver us from evil"

What does Jesus really mean when he speaks of "evil"? From what do we want to be liberated with the statement, "deliver us from evil"?

Certainly sickness is an evil, as are accidents, misfortune, hunger, poverty, homelessness, and unemployment. Nevertheless, liberation from these evils—as we will see—is invoked in the positive with the expression, "give us this day our daily bread."

In the final petition of the Our Father, instead, evil is evoked in its most profound and destructive form: Jesus speaks of the moral evil that is the ultimate root of all other evils. In fact, the Greek term used by Matthew and translated as "evil" is better rendered as "wickedness, malice" or "wicked, malicious."

The Fathers of the Latin Church opted for the neutral "deliver us from wickedness, from evil" during the Mass. Immediately after the recitation of the Our Father, we continue with the prayer, "Deliver us Lord, from every evil and grant us peace in our day. In your mercy keep us free from sin and protect us from all anxiety."

The Fathers of the Greek Church, however, opted for the masculine substantive "deliver us from the evil one," from the malevolent one, from Satan, from the adversary. The two texts from the New Testament that I recalled at the outset share this meaning, from the First Letter of John and from the Second Letter of Paul to the Thessalonians: "You have conquered the evil one; we may be delivered from perverse and wicked people; he will strengthen you and guard you from the evil one." So the term *evil* can be translated in two ways, the meanings of which, in the end, are not opposed; one implies the other.

"Evil": When one speaks about evil and wickedness in the abstract, single transgressions, sins, come immediately to mind — like fraud, homicide, theft, jealousy, vendettas.

In reality, there is an evil more terrible and destructive, constituted by collective transgressions that involve a group, a people, a society — like racism, ethnic wars, the crushing effects of slavery, social injustices, torture. It is more difficult to defend yourself from these evils because they lurk within a culture; they are the DNA of a social group.

Nevertheless, there is an evil, a wickedness even worse that one observes when the wrongdoing not only makes up part of social norms, but when it is legitimated by theories, by ideologies, or by philosophies. In this case the evil is even called "good," the darkness can be called "light." From just this sort of situation of deviance, of structural sin, it is almost impossible to reverse the slippery slope and return toward the good. Consider, for example, the tremendous evil perpetrated in the concentration camps in Auschwitz.

Consequently, Jesus teaches us to cry out to the Father, aggrieved, "deliver us from evil," from the wickedness that besieges each one of us; deliver us from collective aberrations; deliver us, Father, from ideologies that justify and legitimize systematic evil.

The "Evil One": If we read the masculine Greek term—malevolent, wicked, bad—then we find ourselves before another scenario: those who want evil to befall us, who hate us—in other words, the external evil which lay outside of ourselves. The evil internal to ourselves is found in all those destructive feelings and attitudes that gnaw at us and carry us toward evil. I think of depression (often called the "obscure evil"), of discouragement, of bitter pessimism, of the despondency that would make us abandon the way of uprightness and honesty.

Here we notice the continuity between the invocation "deliver us from evil" and the preceding one, "lead us not into temptation."

Temptations, in fact, lead to evil and, when we fall, the evil lacerates the conscience, robs us of peace, renders us contemptible in our own eyes. From such restlessness, from the desire to forget, from disorder in life, in eating and drinking, one can arrive at the escape of drugs and, finally, at despair itself. And it is this great evil from which we ask to be liberated, the evil that would like to put an end to everything.

The "evil one" did not spare Jesus who, before initiating his public life, was approached by the devil. The devil tempted him suggesting to him that yes, he was the Messiah, the Son of God, but through signs of power and dominion ("Command that these stones become loaves of bread . . . throw yourself down from the parapet of the temple," Matthew 4:3, 5) not through the way of humility, meekness, and the cross.

Even Peter, at a certain point, became for Jesus like a wicked person, a tempter who seeks to convince him to renounce the way of the cross, and Jesus responds to him: "Get behind me, Satan!" (Mark 8:33).

Again, when he has already been placed on the cross, Jesus is tempted to come down, fulfilling a portentous gesture: "If you are the Son of God, come down from the cross" (Matthew 27:40).

The fact that temptation and evil might be near to Jesus, during his life and also in the hour of his death, shows how great and terrible is the evil that is near us. Jesus knew well that his disciples would not be spared from the treachery of the evil one and for this, at the Last Supper, he prays to the Father: "Protect them from the evil one" (John 17:15). During the same supper Jesus turns to Peter saying, "Simon, Simon, listen! Satan has demanded to sift all of you like wheat, but I have prayed for you that your own faith may not fail" (Luke 22:31–32a). Certainly the prayer of Jesus will not impede Peter from vacillating, from denying his Master. Nevertheless, it gave him the strength to get back on his feet after the blow.

How Does the Father Deliver Us from Evil?

We ask ourselves: How does the Father deliver us from evil, understood as wickedness, ill will, malignity, and as the evil one, the tempter?

We read in the Gospels that Jesus liberated the men and women of his time from many physical evils, in particular from illnesses:

"Power came out from him and healed all of them" (Luke 6:19). It is the power that we invoke often when we are sick, in order to heal.

The strategy of Jesus is, however, different before the deepest kind of evil, the wickedness of moral evil. It is a rather painful and personal strategy because he himself must bear all of these evils. He allows himself to be flogged and crushed by human wickedness and yet he is victorious, through forgiveness and pardon, offering himself on the cross for us.

That "deliver us from evil" truly has terrible consequences for Jesus, who submerges our wickedness in the sea of his limitless love.

The invocation "deliver us from evil," in its most profound meaning, makes an appeal to the death and resurrection of Jesus. The Lord does not prevent us from feeling the impact of evil in the world; rather, he helps us to enter into it with the faith and hope of one who is certain of victory.

The most serious evil is to succumb in the midst of trial, to lose faith and hope, to despair of one's self. It is from this fate that we ask to be saved. So the Father saves us just as he protected, saved, and liberated Jesus, impeding the definitive victory of the enemy. The Father saves us by giving us the strength to endure the evils of this world like those triumphant in hope. This endurance has everything to do with a profound freedom, neither spectacular nor dramatic, but one that allows us to mysteriously experience the loving nearness of the Father. With this kind of hope we ask him, "deliver us from evil."

Questions for Personal Reflection

1. From which evils should we pray to be freed in our own time?

2. What are the collective evils that weigh most heavily on us and from which we would like to rise again?

Two come to mind.

First of all, *the loss of hope*, the fear of the future. It is a cancer that erodes Western society.

Fear of the future also explains growing conflict, the relentless defense of that which someone has. It explains the fear of giving of oneself, of giving life, of the fall of the birth rate, systematic criticism that extinguishes all creativity. The absence of enthusiasm is a sort of collective evil that is at times justified and that encourages us to seek, at any cost, diversions, distractions, and deafening noise; to prolong one's youth indefinitely so that one need not look the challenges of adult life in the face.

> Deliver us, Father, from fear, from the evil of anxiety, from the evil of too little hope!

A second evil from which we ask to be delivered today as a society is *the prevalence of individual interests* or of group interests against the common good. This dominance is connected to the loss of hope. We no longer have eyes to see the common good—be it of the family or of the city; be it of the nation or of Europe and of the world. Each person struggles to conserve or increase the little or great amount he has, without worrying about anyone else. As a consequence, solidarity is mocked and gestures of sharing are suspect as if they might be importuned by dark self-centered motives. No one wants to risk anymore for a higher good.

It is right, therefore, to pray, "Father, deliver us from this evil, from the dominance of individual interests. Let solidarity triumph and care of our neighbor be the root of every good deed, of every institution that commits itself to the well being of humanity."

In conclusion, I suggest a personal question to which you may respond in silent meditation: If I were to give substance to the prayer "deliver us from evil," what would I give it? From what evils in particular would I like to be delivered?

May the Lord give to us and to all people the hope of victory over evil everywhere we might find it.

※ III ※

Give Us Bread, Forgive Trespasses

AT THE PRISON
OF SAN VITTORE

God, our Father,

you burden yourself with the journey of your children,

giving them what is necessary for living

and opening them to encounter you.

When they err you are ready to pardon.

We thank you for your patient and merciful love.

Help us to place our trust in you

and to learn to be merciful

by forgiving one another.

*T*his evening we face two important petitions of the Our Father, the fourth and the fifth: "Give us this day our daily bread, forgive us our trespasses." Bread and pardon are two fundamental necessities for human existence. *Bread*, with everything that it means — food, health, home, work, freedom; *pardon*, with everything that it involves — good relations, reconciliation in the family, in the city, in society, and also heartfelt peace between persons and institutions.

Let us consider three gospel texts that can help us in our reflection.

"Our ancestors ate the manna in the wilderness; as it is written, 'He gave them bread from heaven to eat.'" Then Jesus said to them, "Very truly, I tell you, it was not Moses who gave you the bread from heaven; but it is my Father who gives you the true bread from heaven. For the bread of God is that which comes down from heaven and gives life to the world." They said to him, "Sir, give us this bread always." Jesus said to them, "I am the bread of life. Whoever comes to me will never be hungry, and whoever believes in me will never be thirsty" (John 6:31–35).

"For if you forgive others their trespasses, your heavenly Father will also forgive you; but if you do not forgive others, neither will your Father forgive your trespasses" (Matthew 6:14–15).

Then Peter came and said to him, "Lord, if another member of the church sins against me, how often should I forgive? As many as seven times?" Jesus said to him, "Not seven times, but, I tell you, seventy-seven times" (Matthew 18:21–22).

Let us pause to consider these two petitions of the Our Father from this very meaningful place, the Prison of San Vittore, and at this moment let us think about all the other penal institutions of our diocese (the one belonging to Opera, and the neighboring ones in Monza, Busto, Arsizio, and Lecco). They are places where many of the emblematic sufferings of our society cross paths, places of pain and repression, of sadness. They are places that know the kind of despair that pushes people to make tragic, often fatal gestures. In these penal institutions, the material bread about which the prayer the Our Father speaks is not lacking, even if it is a bit stale. What is lacking, however, is freedom and familial affection. As a friend who greeted me at the beginning emphasized, in the name of all, "We, too, are hungry for bread and peace." How much hunger there is here for freedom, home, family, and peace!

San Vittore is a place where the conflicts within society are reflected, the ones that turn persons against one another. However, if looked at with greater perspective, it is a place in which reconciliation and rehabilitation should be propitiated, in which journeys toward conversion and grace should be achieved. Consequently, prison is one of the most affecting symbolic arenas of our society. Every time that I come to visit you, I am deeply moved. Here I fulfill more than ever my service as bishop. And I like to remember that from this very prison I initiated, in 1981, my first pastoral visit of the diocese, believing in fact that it might be a central place of the city and of the region. In succession, I have returned on various occasions, in particular to celebrate the first Christmas Mass with the sincere desire to express my best wishes to the inmates and to all those who work on their behalf. Last Christmas you gave me a large notebook with your signatures that I will deliver shortly to the Pope; then I received another one from the Opera prison, and this evening I would like, in prayer, to remember especially the thousands of people who signed those notebooks.

While I greet each one of you with affection—both male and female inmates, prison guards, civil and military servants, volunteers, priest and sister chaplains—I greet also all those who are listening by radio or watching on television. I am pleased to think that realized in this moment is something of the relationship between prison and society that is very important for the humanization of prison, in order to effect greater communication between prison and civil society.

Again, by way of introduction, I thank you for having prepared for the reflection on the Our Father through the explanation in my pastoral letter, "Return to the Father of all," something offered to you by the chaplains on each Sunday of Lent leading up to Easter. I am speaking, therefore, to a group that has been meditating attentively on the mystery of the paternity of God, a group that could teach us, also me, many things about the Father who is in heaven, about the temptations that we have all neglected, about the longing for him. I am conscious of the Lenten journey in which you are engaged, as well as the symbolic gifts that you have presented to me—a book that recalls the symbols of

Hebrew thought, and the figure of Jesus in prayer. I will let myself be inspired by these symbols too.

"Give us this day our daily bread"

The invocation, "give us this day our daily bread," occupies a central place in the prayer Jesus taught us because it is the fourth of seven petitions, three before and three after.

The first three directly regard the Father who is in heaven: hallowed be your name, your Kingdom come, your will be done. The three successive petitions following the request for bread regard us and take as a point of departure human needs: need for forgiveness, support during times of trial, freedom from evil.

WHAT DOES ONE ASK
WITH THE FOURTH PETITION?

Certainly everything that has to do with physical, biological life—that has to do with our everyday necessities like food, health, home, work.

Nevertheless, we ask for even more: that which allows us to survive as persons, with the dignity of men and women, with our characteristic hunger for authentic values, search for joy and truth, our quest for the meaning of life.

The word "bread" has both meanings. In the text of chapter 6 of John, recalled at the beginning, the bread indicates either the food that satisfied the Hebrews in the desert, "he gave them bread from heaven to eat"; or the food of the soul, "the bread from heaven, the true bread, that gives life to the world."

What is the spiritual bread that we ask for in particular? With the nontechnical language of the layman, one might call it the meaning of life. Something that gives meaning to our being in the world, that allows us to survive in spite of the trials and the difficult and dark moments; that which makes us hope, love, fight for our dignity.

With religious language, the spiritual bread is the bread of faith and hope: with the invocation "give us our daily bread," we implore the Father for the grace of the Holy Spirit, Jesus himself, as gift and guardian of the true meaning of life. We ask that Jesus might be near to us as a friend, the one who never leaves us alone, Jesus in the Mass, in the eucharistic communion, in the tabernacle.

WHO IS ABLE TO ADDRESS
THIS PETITION TO THE FATHER?

In the first place, the one who is hungry. I think especially of all the people and all the categories of persons, also those in our midst, that lack the most indispensable things to live, like food; peoples oppressed by misery and hunger, who appeal to the opulence of the West to be helped and saved.

But physical hunger is not sufficient to render this prayer universal. The one who does not lack bread today can make his own petition to the Father, and in a deep sense, on three conditions.

The first: that he recognize the need for something and he might not have the pride to want to be self-sufficient. There are persons who glory in not needing anything or anyone, in not being dependent: the Gospel calls these persons, "the rich," those people who love power, success, and wealth over everything, and pretend to subjugate all else.

To ask for bread, even if there is bread on the table, it is necessary to feel in some way poor, full of desire, of expectation.

The first condition is not enough. We must add a second to it: the one who has desires must *know that there is a Father who cares about him and looks on him with love.* In this way this prayer becomes the prayer of the children of God, who entrust themselves to the Father who is in the heavens, not to dispense themselves from work but to do it in a just, honest, and serene manner, with the certainty that a Father thinks about them, does not forget them. It is, therefore, an invocation that enlarges the heart. I can speak about myself to the One that listens to me and thinks about me.

The third condition to ask for bread is more demanding: *he must have the Kingdom of God and God's will as his primary interest.* He must place before all values, truth, love, and the justice of the Kingdom in the certainty that when one desires the Kingdom, all else will be given to him besides (see Matthew 6:33). In other words, the one who bets his life on the Kingdom of God recites this prayer profoundly and knows that

he can ask everything of God and expect everything from God.

We recognize ourselves perhaps too easily
in the first condition (we are needy and we ask
for help from another); we see ourselves a bit in
the second (we know that a Father thinks about
us); we find it difficult, however, to enter into
the third condition, into having as our first
desire the Kingdom of God, justice, and truth.
Yet we catch a glimpse; we intuit that, in particular, this third condition introduces us into a
peace and serenity that nothing can obfuscate.

The fourth petition of the Our Father is
then an invitation to check our priorities against
those of the Kingdom of God. What really lies
in our hearts? If it is bread alone, we can still
recite this prayer, even if a bit distanced from it.
If that which lay in our hearts is truth, honesty,
justice, goodness, friendship, then our order of
values is correct and our prayer is authentic.

"Forgive us our trespasses as we forgive those who trespass against us"

Let us consider now the next petition, the fifth, that asks pardon: "Forgive us our trespasses as we forgive those who trespass against us."

WHAT DOES ONE ASK FOR?

Reconciliation with God, but a reconciliation that passes through reconciliation between us.

This petition is crucial for social and civil life, for the city and humanity, since the moment we find ourselves without reconciliation, we will never have peace on earth.

It is interesting to note that one invokes not only the pardon of the Father, almost as if everything might happen between God and us, as well as the *capacity to know how to forgive and the capacity* – perhaps even more difficult – *to let oneself forgive.* As we recited in the initial prayer of this meeting, we invoke peace of the heart, social reconciliation.

We are then before the request of a primary blessing, be it for the conscience or for the network of daily relationships; a blessing without which bread can be stale and indigestible. We could, in fact, have all the riches of the world, but if there is not peace, harmony in the family, trust among friends, if there are offenses and offenders who look at each other with diffidence and hate, then that wealth does not produce anything but aridity and loneliness.

And it is left to precisely this place, the prison, to say that no sentence is enough, no punishment suffices if reconciliation does not grow, if there is not the capacity to meet again as brothers and sisters gathered at the same table.

Who Is Able to Address the Fifth Petition to the Father?

Obviously the one who is ready to forgive and to receive the forgiveness of others, the one who recognizes how meaningful it is to forgive and to be forgiven.

The passage of the Gospel According to Matthew is very clear in purpose: "If you forgive others their trespasses, your heavenly Father will forgive you. But if you do not forgive others, neither will your Father forgive your trespasses" (Matthew 6:14–15).

And the other text, also from Matthew, actually affirms that one ought to forgive not up to seven times, but up to seventy times seven times (see Matthew 18:21–22). If we calculate the minutes that make up a day, we realize that seventy times seven times means to forgive every three minutes. The forgiveness received is, therefore, the substance of daily life.

We must forgive one another many things, the many persons that disappoint us; those that don't respond to our expectations or that leave us alone in our need. We must continually express reconciliation in order to make peace in our hearts. Forgiveness is an essential blessing, intrinsic to Christianity; indeed, it is a blessing without which human life is unthinkable.

Accordingly, on the occasion of the Jubilee, a request has been raised—at an international level—of the remission, or at least the drastic reduction, of the foreign debt of poor countries. For this, you who are incarcerated raise the request of forgiveness and reconciliation through the realization of some measures of clemency. All this originates with the fifth petition of the Our Father. I mentioned earlier the notebook with the letter that you gave me on Christmas Day so that I might present it to the Pope. That letter gives one pause to reflect because it is born from prayer, and I want to quote from part of it:

> For some time now a sincere desire has arisen in us to ask forgiveness, with his voice and with his heart, of the persons whom we have offended, to return to God the Father, to reenter the human community, to remove from our bodies the clothes of the prodigal son. We are determined to clothe ourselves again with the clothing of Jesus, who was humble and full of peace, just and good with all, arrested, condemned and crucified for us.

With such a resolution, gestures of clemency and remission are invoked.

Analogous words echo in the letter from the inmates in the prison of Opera:

> Also we in prison, like you in your numerous trips and certainly in your numerous prayers, breathe an air of

internationality. Men of every tongue, people, and nation live here side by side, in expectation of the longed-for liberation of body and spirit, and these are the same men that assure you of their concrete commitment to direct their own future course toward the reconstruction of civil and ethical values, wherever there will be doors open and opportunities afforded of reinsertion into the living fabric of society.

I make myself the interpreter of such appeals when I say that they show how forgiveness is an essential blessing not only of Christianity but for all of society.

We all know that to forgive is extremely difficult and it is even more difficult to be forgiven. Not by chance, the Our Father, in the simple petition, "forgive us our trespasses as we forgive those who trespass against us" contains—it seems to me—an implicit reference to the cry of Jesus on the cross: "Father, forgive them" (Luke 23:34). While being tortured and crucified, Jesus finds words of forgiveness.

Questions for Personal Reflection

After having attempted to explain a bit the fourth and fifth petition, I pose three questions that will help each one of us to examine ourselves.

1. In daily necessities, do I look with trust to the Father who is in heaven, or do I close myself in solitude and pessimism? Do I turn in on myself, closing my eyes and ears to any thought of the Father?

2. Am I convinced that the fabric of life is woven with gestures of forgiveness, forgiveness given and received? Am I convinced that without forgiveness life becomes a kind of hell?

3. (The third question regards in particular those who are in the listening audience.) What can I do so that the reality of the prison might be more deeply understood in society and in the Church, and so that alternative measures to prison might be

studied efficaciously, ones that might be about forgiveness and reconciliation?

In order to bring ourselves to a moment of silent meditation, I invite all those present in this rotunda to repeat with me the abbreviated version of one of the most beautiful psalms in the entire Psalter:

Have mercy on me, God, in your goodness;
in your abundant compassion blot out
    my offense.
Against you alone have I sinned;
I have done such evil in your sight
that you are just in your sentence,
blameless when you condemn.

True, I was born guilty,
a sinner, even as my mother conceived me.
Still, you insist on sincerity of heart;
in my inmost being teach me wisdom.
Turn away your face from my sins;
blot out all my guilt.

A clean heart create for me, God;
renew in me a steadfast spirit.

Do not drive me from your presence,
nor take from me your holy spirit.
Restore my joy in your salvation;
sustain in me a willing spirit.

Make Zion prosper in your good pleasure;
rebuild the walls of Jerusalem.
(see Psalm 51:3, 6–8, 11–14, 20)

✳ IV ✳

Thy Will
Be Done

AT THE MONASTERY
OF THE POOR CLARES

Your will, O God,

is the salvation of every person;

in order to accomplish it you sent your Son

who died and rose for us.

Make us understand the mystery

of your love;

give us an expansive heart

capable of accepting your desires

and of modeling our choices on them.

Open us to accept your Word,

to recognize it as light for our path,

as a gift

able to give meaning to our life.

Through Christ our Lord.

Amen.

I selected two gospel texts to introduce us into meditation on the third petition of the Our Father: "thy will be done," that "will" that Jesus often mentioned during his earthly life declaring that it was his food, that he came into the world to do the will of God.

> Then he said to them, "I am deeply grieved, even to death; remain here, and stay awake with me." And going a little farther, he threw himself on the ground and prayed, "My Father, if it is possible, let this cup pass from me; yet,

not what I want but what you want."
Then he came to the disciples and
found them sleeping; and he said to
Peter, "So, could you not stay awake
with me one hour? Stay awake and
pray that you may not come into the
time of trial; the spirit indeed is willing, but the flesh is weak." Again he
went away for the second time and
prayed, "My Father, if this cannot pass
unless I drink it, your will be done."
Again he came and found them sleeping, for their eyes were heavy. So leav-
ing them again, he went away and
prayed for a third time, saying the same
words (Matthew 26:38–44).

"Everything that the Father gives me
will come to me, and anyone who
comes to me I will never drive away;
for I have come down from heaven,
not to do my own will, but the will of
him who sent me. And this is the will
of him who sent me, that I should lose
nothing of all that he has given me,

but raise it up on the last day. This is indeed the will of my Father, that all who see the Son and believe in him may have eternal life; and I will raise them up on the last day" (John 6:37–40).

This evening I find myself in the Monastery of the Poor Clares, in a place where one places the will of God before all else, in the tradition of Francis of Assisi and Saint Clare. It is also a place where one prays for the entire city and for the many hardships suffered in the city. Beyond that, this house, situated in Little Martyrs Piazza, is not far from where, on October 20, 1944, a bomb destroyed a school and killed 184 children and 17 adults. We remember, therefore, a great tragedy and we are invited to pray for all the suffering of the world, in particular for the suffering caused by war.

What Does One Ask with the Third Petition?

In order to understand what we are asking for as we pray the third petition of the Our

Father, we must analyze it word by word: the will of God; be done, be fulfilled; on earth as it is in heaven.

The Will of God

The *will of God* is first of all the comprehensive plan of God for the universe and history. It is the marvelous plan through which the Father, "destined us for adoption as his children through Jesus Christ, according to the good pleasure of his will," as Paul writes in the Letter to the Ephesians (1:5). And again Paul affirms, "he has made known to us the mystery of his will . . . as a plan for the fullness of time, to gather up all things in him, things in heaven and things on earth" (9a, 10). It is this plan, this will of God, that we ask might be fulfilled.

The same expression, "thy will be done," can, nevertheless, refer also to any singular expression of the will of God. We remember, for example, that Jesus, after having recounted the parable of the lost sheep that was sought out by the shepherd with a love that would leave the ninety-nine sheep on the hills, concludes, "So it is not the will of your Father in heaven that one of these little ones should be lost" (Matthew 18:14). The will of God is the salvation of the little ones.

Another moment of expression of the will of the Father, we find in Jesus' exclamation, "I thank you, Father, Lord of heaven and earth, because you have hidden these things from the wise and the intelligent and have revealed them to infants; yes, Father, for such was your gracious will" (Matthew 11:25–26). The will of God is that the gospel might be revealed to the little ones.

We could say then, that the will of the Father is his *efficacious love for us*, it is the plan that God carries forward, constantly working out our salvation. It is the stupendous project recalled by Jesus in the discourse after the multiplication of the loaves in the text cited at the beginning: "this is indeed the will of my Father, that all who see the Son and believe in him may have eternal life" (John 6:40).

BE DONE, BE FULFILLED

Thy will be done. Exegetes ask themselves, "By whom must it be done?" What is the intended subject of the passive verb *be done*? Is it God who does it or us men and women here on the earth?

From an examination of the context of such a word in the Gospels, it seems that both meanings are valid. This "will" must be done first of all by God; it is he who fulfills his plan of salvation. So the invocation becomes an auspice, an augury: Fulfill, O Father, your plan of salvation for the world. Let your Kingdom come! Reunite all in Jesus Christ. Prepare the fullness of life for your children!

However, we too fulfill the will of God day after day; his will is also our task and, in this case, the invocation is a prayer because the Father sustains our fragile will, so that we can carry out in every case whatever the Father wants from us. Jesus emphasizes this well in Matthew 7:21: "Not everyone who says to me, 'Lord, Lord,' will enter the kingdom of heaven, but only the one who does the will of my Father in heaven." And in Matthew 12:50: "For whoever does the will of my Father in heaven is my brother and sister and mother." A beautiful thought, very powerful and consoling. We then ask to know how to fulfill the divine will in the sense of Mary's response to the angel: "Let it be with me according to your word" (Luke 1:38).

ON EARTH AS IT IS IN HEAVEN

As it is in heaven. Here we're not talking about heaven as the space above the earth, but of heaven as the place where God reveals himself in fullness to the angels, to the saints, the place where God reigns without obstacles and without resistances, where his will is followed perfectly, without ambiguity. It is the celestial Jerusalem, the glorified Christ.

We ask that what is done in heaven might also be done on earth. The original Greek text sounds a bit different from the Italian translation, "as in heaven, so be it on earth." It is a bit excessive to think that the will of God might be done on earth in the same way in which it is done in heaven! It would be better to translate it, "as in heaven, *also* on earth," to indicate that we are to imitate in some way that which happens in heaven. We must begin by doing the will of the Father so that heaven might come to the earth, so that the Kingdom already realized in the Risen

Christ, in the angels and saints, might come, might be realized again among us, until the salvific plan of God is completely fulfilled.

I would like to note that the comparative formula "as in heaven also on earth" or "as in heaven so be it on earth" can rightly be the introduction to all three of the first petitions of the Our Father:

> Hallowed be thy name,
> as it is in heaven also on earth;
> thy Kingdom come,
> as it is in heaven also on earth;
> your stupendous plan of salvation
> might be done,
> as it is in heaven also on earth.

In the Our Father, Jesus invites us to look courageously to the place where God reveals himself in fullness, to pray in the light of definitive realities. The journey of men and women is not an uncertain wandering in darkness. Jesus makes us understand that this journey, like the history of the world, has its point of reference in the plan of divine love. The Father has realized his plan in the celestial Jerusalem and has begun to fulfill it on earth: heaven begins to come to earth.

Who Is Able to Make This Invocation?

After having sought to explain the riches contained in the petition, "thy will be done as in heaven also on earth," I must ask myself who is really able to pray like this. The answer is simple.

JESUS IS ABLE TO PRAY LIKE THIS

In his life and his death, Jesus is always thinking about the will of the Father. "My food is to do the will of him who sent me and to complete his work" (John 4:34). "I have come down from heaven, not to do my own will, but the will of him who sent me" (John 6:38).

Only Jesus can perfectly do this petition, this prayer. Most importantly, he repeats it in a sublime way during his agony when, faced with the fear of death, he exclaims, "My Father, if it is possible, let this cup pass from me; yet not what I want but what you want." And again, "My Father, if this cannot pass unless I drink it, your will be done!" (Matthew 26:39, 42).

EVERY BELIEVER IS ABLE TO PRAY LIKE THIS

Adopting then these words from the lips of Jesus, every believer can repeat this invocation in moments of trial, of difficulty, of suffering — in the moments in which is it difficult to do the will of God.

Let us look at a lovely page from the Acts of the Apostles that follows the same theme. Paul was going up to Jerusalem, where he would be imprisoned, and the Christians of Caesarea were attempting to stop him in order to impede the dramatic conclusion of his apostolic ministry. But Paul responded, "'What are you doing, weeping and breaking my heart? For I am ready not only to be bound but even to die in Jerusalem for the name of the Lord Jesus.' Since he would not be persuaded, we remained silent except to say, 'The Lord's will be done'" (21:13–14).

It is a prayer that has been repeated an infinite number of times in the lives of countless believers, men and women, in the difficult moments of life—a prayer that alleviated great pain, that comforted many hearts. I've also listened to people very gravely ill and infirm, exclaim with a whisper, "O God, thy will be done!" The apostle Peter exhorts Christians to resist during persecution, remembering that, "for it is better to suffer for doing good, if suffering should be God's will, than to suffer for doing evil" (1 Peter 3:17), and he adds, "Therefore, let those suffering in accordance with God's will entrust themselves to a faithful Creator, while continuing to do good" (4:19).

It is a prayer that becomes particularly insistent in times of trial, during the dark night of the soul, in the desert, in anguish, because it brings peace and it allows us to read in these situations of suffering the plan of God. John XXIII, for his motto, chose the expression, *Oboedientia et pax*, obedience and peace—peace, in fact, from knowing oneself as given over, entrusted, to the will of God.

THE ONE WHO SUFFERS
IS ABLE TO PRAY LIKE THIS

"Thy will be done on earth as it is in heaven" is also the invocation of the one who suffers because this will is not yet fulfilled in the world. This is the prayer of those who suffer from injustice, from cruelty, from prevarications, from exploitation. It is the prayer of the vulnerable and the poor, of those who hunger and thirst for justice. In that sense, it is a universal prayer. Make evident, O Father, your truth, your will, your justice.

It is a prayer of intercession, habitual in a monastery. An intercession made in the heartfelt longing for the fulfillment of the holy will of God in the world, in the desire that the shameful stains that deface the earth and bring it to ruin might disappear.

The Joyful Believer
Is Able to Pray Like This

Finally, it is the invocation of the believer in moments of joy. Paul begins his Letter to the Colossians with a hymn of joy: "For in him all the fullness was pleased to dwell, and through him God was pleased to reconcile to himself all things, whether on earth or in heaven, by making peace through the blood of his cross" (1:19–20). The apostle takes pleasure in the fulfillment of the will of God; he rejoices because God's will is done. We, too, can give praise to the Father, saying with joy "thy will be done" every time we contemplate the realization of some aspect or expression of the will of God in us or in the world.

This is the invocation of those who commit themselves through hard work so that justice, honesty, and peace triumph. It is the prayer of the "Peace Makers." In that regard I like to cite the comment of Francis of Assisi:

> Thy will be done on earth as it is in heaven: so that we love you with all our heart, always thinking about you, always desiring you with all our soul, orienting ourselves to you so that every intention of our mind is directed to you, seeking in everything your honor with all our strength, expending all the energies and senses of our body and soul to the service of your love and for nothing else, and so that we love our neighbor as ourselves, carrying everyone with all our power to your love, taking pleasure in the well being of the

other as in our own, suffering along with them in their suffering, not offending anyone, seeking never to hurt anyone.

It is, therefore, a very active prayer, made by those who expend their energies, by those who work on behalf of others. Saint Francis interprets this invocation of the Our Father in a practical way that explains the will of God according to the double commandment to love.

We can affirm that, if on the one hand, it is a passive invocation in which one must entrust oneself to God, it is, on the other, a challenge to love our brothers and sisters, to take pleasure in the well being of others, and to relieve our neighbor from the sufferings he or she bears.

Questions for Personal Reflection

At this point I would like to offer some questions for our own personal reflection.

1. What, in me, is opposed to the will of God, understood as either the universal plan of salvation or as God's will for me

in particular moments in life? What blocks me or impedes me from walking along the way of the will of the Father, that is the way of peace?

2.   Do I find joy in God's will? A saint once said, "Will of God, my paradise." Is the will of God really my paradise, as it is in heaven is it also on earth?

3.   (The third question I ask, in particular, of young people.) Do I seek the will of God as I plan my own future? Do I hear the call of God, that is his will, in my life?

The religious women who live in this monastery answered yes to the call of the Lord. They took his will seriously in their lives and they teach us, consequently, to embrace with joy our own call in order to make of our own life an act of obedience to the plan of God's love.

Conclusion

It seems to me right and good to conclude with another saying of Saint Francis, one that shows how he would depend in all things on the will of the Father. I've drawn it from his testament: "And after the Lord gave me some brothers, no one showed me what I should do. But the same Most High One revealed to me that I should live the norm of the Holy Gospel and I, with few and simple words, wrote it, and my lord, the Pope confirmed it for me." The relationship between the charismatic understanding of the will of God ("the Most High One revealed it to me") and the conformity with the Church ("the Pope confirmed it for me") is significant. The will of God is always realized in full communion with the Church.

And in order to know the will of God, let us allow this prayer of Saint Francis to resound within us:

> Omnipotent, eternal, just
> and merciful God,
> allow us lowly ones to do by your grace,
> that which we know you want,
> and to desire always that which
>   pleases you,
> so that, interiorly purified, illuminated
> and enflamed by the fire of the Holy Spirit,

we can follow in the footsteps of your Son
and return to you, O Most High One,
with the help of your grace alone.

❊ V ❊

Thy Kingdom Come

AT ST. MARY BELTRADE
PARISH CHURCH

Your Kingdom, O God,

is the certain destination

of humankind's journey.

Make us ready to embrace

this announcement of life and hope,

so that we might model

our decisions and deliberations on it.

Guide our choices

that they might conform to your Word

and that they might originate

from a true process of conversion.

Through Christ our Lord.

Amen.

*A*fter having explained the petitions of the Our Father beginning from contexts and places a bit out of the ordinary — the hospital, the prison, a cloistered convent — we conclude the Lenten catechesis in the parish of St. Mary Beltrade, that is, in a setting where one finds the ordinary life of the People of God. The parish, as such, is a school of sanctity and, in it, we all feel called to be sons and daughters of God and saints.

I would like to warmly greet all the faithful of this community and thank the Provost for his words of welcome. And I would like also to thank all those who have followed us and those who wrote me to say how touched they were by my reflections. It has been wonderful to prepare ourselves together to live intensely Holy Week and Easter.

"Thy Kingdom come" is the central invocation of prayer taught to us by Jesus, and three gospel passages from Matthew will help us to understand it.

> From that time Jesus began to proclaim, "Repent, for the kingdom of heaven has come near" (4:17).

> "Therefore do not worry saying, 'What will we eat?' or 'What will we drink?' or 'What will we wear?' For it is the Gentiles who strive for all these things; and indeed your heavenly Father knows that you need all these things. But strive first for the kingdom of God and his righteousness, and all these things will be given to you as well.
>
> "So do not worry about tomorrow, for tomorrow will bring worries of its

own. Today's trouble is enough for today" (6:31–34).

"Not everyone who says to me, 'Lord, Lord,' will enter the kingdom of heaven, but only the one who does the will of my Father in heaven" (7:21).

"Thy Kingdom come"

I confess to feeling a bit of embarrassment in explaining the petition "thy Kingdom come"; I have meditated on it many times in my life, yet it is as if I might have always been placed before something that escapes me, that goes beyond my words. To understand, for example, what Jesus meant to say with "thy Kingdom come," it would be necessary to enter into his mind and heart. It would be necessary to make his desires our own in order to understand what that fire was that he wanted to bring to the earth: "I came to bring fire to the earth, and how I wish it were already kindled!" (Luke 12:49). Or another exclamation of his: "I have eagerly desired to eat this Passover with you before I suffer" (Luke 22:15).

"Thy Kingdom come" is like the synthesis of the desires that animated Jesus: it is the fire that he had inside himself. Not by chance in the Synoptic Gospels does the word *kingdom* appear at least ninety times on Jesus' lips.

I mentioned before the fact that it is a key petition in the Our Father because all the other petitions are connected to it.

The coming of the Kingdom is a concrete way with which the holy name of God is glorified. The Kingdom comes through the fulfillment of the will of the Father, as it is in heaven so also on earth; those who seek first the Kingdom can await with trust their daily bread, they learn to forgive by entering into the certainty of the forgiveness of the Father. We can also be tempted by desperation, and thus we are in need of the support of the heavenly Father ("lead us not into temptation"); we need to be liberated from sin or from evil.

Therefore, all the invocations are connected to one another, but the one about the Kingdom is the center of prayer, the point of reference for the others.

I propose to explain the petition by responding to three questions: What do we ask for when we say that the Kingdom of the Father might come? How or where does the Kingdom come? Who is capable of making this petition his or her own?

What Does One Ask with the Second Petition?

The word *kingdom*, in Greek, has different meanings. In fact, it can be translated with *sovereignty* to indicate *the legal condition by which God the Father can be proclaimed sovereign over the world.* It is a condition that belongs to him beginning with creation, that is, always. In this sense, the Kingdom doesn't come; rather, it already is, since the beginning, since creation itself.

This word can, however, also be translated — as we usually do — with *reign*, not with sovereignty. "Reign" emphasizes the *concrete territory in which God exercises his sovereignty*, the places, the space in which God fully manifests his dominion. This is how the Kingdom is in heaven and will come on the earth. The final stage will be realized when the dominion of God will be definitively recognized and proclaimed in the entire universe.

But the same Greek word can be translated as "lordship," to describe therefore *the activity through which the Father takes visible possession of the world*. The activity that has its culmination in the incarnation, passion, death, and resurrection of Jesus, and that continues in the life of the Church, in history, until the return of the Lord, where he will obtain his full development and his total visibility.

The Fathers of the Church add here a further meaning. Saint Cyprian, for example, writes, "It is also possible that the kingdom of God might mean Christ in person, he whom we invoke with our everyday wishes, he whose coming we insist should hasten with our expectation. Since he is our resurrection and because in him we are resurrected, so too can be the Kingdom of God, because in him we too will reign." So the Kingdom is Jesus himself, and "thy Kingdom come" means, "Come, Lord Jesus!"

The object of the prayer is the Kingdom not so much in the first meaning but in the other three. One asks that the confines within which truth, justice, love, and peace triumph might expand and that might happen starting with Jesus' activities and might be continued in his disciples. One asks that the Lord Jesus himself might come to proclaim the victory of goodness and holiness.

The Kingdom of God, therefore, has to do with the Church, even if it doesn't identify itself with it. On this point we recall a passage from John Paul II's encyclical *Redemptoris Missio,* where he speaks at length about the relationship between the Kingdom and the Church:

> One may not separate the Kingdom from the Church. It is true that the Church is not an end unto herself, since she is ordered toward the Kingdom of God of which she is seed, sign and instrument. Yet, while remaining distinct from Christ and from the Kingdom, the Church is inextricably linked to both. Christ endowed the Church, his body, from the fullness of the benefits and the means of salvation. The Holy Spirit dwells in her, enlivens her with his gifts and charisms, sanctifies, guides and renews her continually. The Church derives from this a unique and singular relationship, that, though not excluding

the work of Christ and of the Holy Spirit outside the visible confines of the Church, confers on her a specific and necessary role" (n. 17).

The petition "thy Kingdom come" doesn't refer specifically to the Church, but it is expressly linked with the coming of the Church, with the expansion of the Church in the world.

However, it seems important we understand that one asks for something total and definitive even if it comes gradually and by steps. For example, one doesn't ask only that the Church might expand, but that the faith might deepen, that sinners might convert — that is part of it, but there is much more. One asks that the present world marked by ambiguity and wickedness might come to end, that the true order of things might triumph, that God might be all in all. It is truly a universal prayer, one that embraces everything. As Saint Paul affirms, "Then comes the end, when he hands over the kingdom to God the Father, after he has destroyed every ruler and every authority and power" (1 Corinthians 15:24).

The invocation of the Kingdom involves all that is desirable, all that concerns the plan and mystery of God; so the subject of the request is vast, indeed. Nevertheless, each one of us can fulfill the petition in part, each according to his or her experience; and we can explain it by responding to the second question.

HOW AND WHERE DOES THE KINGDOM OF GOD COME?

The Kingdom of God comes in every act through which God shows himself Lord of the world and of history.

It began to come with power, especially in the life of Jesus who initiated his ministry with the exhortation, "Repent, for the kingdom of heaven has come near" (Matthew 4:17). And during his life, he affirmed, "But if it is by the Spirit of God that I cast out demons, then the kingdom of God has come to you" (Matthew 12:28). To someone who asked him, "When will the kingdom of God come?" he responded, "The kingdom of God is not coming with things that can be observed; nor will they say, 'Look, here it is!' or, 'There it is!' For, in fact, the kingdom of God is among you" (Luke 17:20–21).

The Kingdom that comes with Jesus continues to come today through the actions of his disciples, through the actions of the Church
prompted by the Spirit. The Kingdom comes in
prayer, in the Eucharist; and is coming at this
moment in meditation. It comes everywhere
someone fulfills the will of the Father. It also
comes in sickness, in pain, and in suffering
accepted with humility. It comes in every sincere
joy and in every gesture of sharing. It comes in
every act of love, of truth, and of justice. It
comes, therefore, even until this moment, even if
it will come in fullness only at the end of time.

And I hasten to emphasize that the Kingdom
comes in human activities like these, just as it is
already manifested in the life of Jesus, that is, in
commitment, humility, and service. For that
reason, the petition "thy kingdom come"
should not make us think about a clamorous
reversal of history. A contemporary exegete said
it well:

> The one who expects a kingdom of
> God that first will overturn the present
> moment will be disappointed. The one
> who understands the beauty of a God

that shares in our lives, will instead feel
renewed. Things remain the same, only
our way of looking at them changes.
The miracle of the kingdom is in the
first place, even if not only, interior
change (Bruno Maggioni, *Padre nostro*,
Vita e Pensiero, Milano, pp. 51–52).

WHO AUTHENTICALLY PRAYS, "THY KINGDOM COME"?

Can we respond to the third question like
this: the one who prays authentically saying,
thy kingdom come?

The one who can pray authentically does
not blindly expect that goodness will triumph
on the earth or that injustice might be defeated
through a clamorous reversal of fortunes. The
one who can pray authentically for the Kingdom is the one who has become a disciple of
Jesus and has understood the humble and poor
manner with which Jesus realizes the dominion
of God in history. In other words, those who
pray authentically have placed all hope in Jesus
and recognize in him and in his humility the
true manifestation of the Father, and have

altered their own ideas about the divine majesty, learning to see divinity even in the mystery of the cross.

The one who has, up to this point, become a disciple of Jesus doesn't allow himself or herself to be taken up by everyday worries, according to the gospel teaching, "Therefore do not worry, saying, 'What will we eat?' or 'What will we drink?' or 'What will we wear?' . . . Strive first for the kingdom of God and his righteousness, and all these things will be given to you as well" (Matthew 6:31, 33). Therefore, the one who prays authentically for the Kingdom knows to place in the Father's hands every worry about the present and the future, because he or she knows that God is a loving Father who provides for everyone, who loves everyone like his own children, and who wants to establish his Kingdom.

The one who prays authentically "thy Kingdom come" remembers the words of Saint Paul: "For the kingdom of God is not food and drink but of righteousness and peace and joy in the Holy Spirit" (Romans 14:17). The Kingdom of God, in fact, is the fruit of the work of the Holy Spirit in us, and the Spirit moves in the sense of the gospel beatitudes, on whose gifts (wisdom,

understanding, counsel, knowledge, piety, forti-
tude, fear of God) and on whose fruits (love,
bounty, moderation, self-control, courtesy, meekness, good humor, joviality, and peace) we have
amply meditated this past year. Finally, the one
who prays authentically trusts in the Holy
Spirit and does the will of the Father: "Not
everyone who says to me, 'Lord, Lord,' will
enter the kingdom of heaven, but only the one
who does the will of my Father in heaven"
(Matthew 7:21).

In order to clarify better still what true
desire for the Kingdom is, I want to cite a
meaningful passage from the *Catechism of the
Catholic Church*, on the subject of this petition of
the Our Father:

> By a discernment according to the Spirit,
> Christians have to distinguish between
> the growth of the Kingdom and the
> progress of the culture and society in
> which they are involved. This distinction
> is not a separation. The vocation of men
> and women to eternal life does not sup-
> press but actually reinforces the duty of
> all to put into action in this world the

energies and the means received from the Creator to serve justice and peace (n. 2820).

The one who prays with authenticity for the coming of the Kingdom works for the progress of humanity, for culture, for civility, and for peace.

I tried to explain, at least in part, that this invocation—as you have already seen—goes beyond us and whose meaning we will understand only in the fullness of the Kingdom. Already now, however, it nourishes our prayer if we repeat it with great hope.

Questions for Personal Reflection

I conclude by proposing three questions that will help us first to examine ourselves in the moment of silence and then also in conversation among ourselves.

1. What feelings does the expression "Kingdom of God" awaken in me? Are they similar to the feelings Jesus had in his heart while he taught the disciples the Our Father? The matter at hand suggests a comparison

between what comes to mind for me when I hear the expression "Kingdom of God" with what came to mind for Jesus when he spoke about it.

2. When saying "thy Kingdom come," do I know I can conquer my fears and entrust my every worry to the Father who knows everything and provides everything?

3. Do I allow myself to be guided by the power of the Holy Spirit in my prayer and in my life, the same Spirit that makes me walk in the ways of the gospel beatitudes and so establishes the Kingdom? Do I entrust myself to the power of the Spirit that makes the Kingdom come already in the simple activities of my daily life?

TRANSLATOR'S
CONCLUSION

As pilgrims, we have responded to the Holy Father's call to see things in the perspective of Christ. Aided by Cardinal Martini's reflections on the prayer Jesus taught us, we have embarked together on a spiritual journey to places new and old, places that encourage and challenge us, places that invite compassion and foster faith. By penetrating the depths of this most familiar of all prayers, we have tried to enter more deeply into the richness of Jesus' feelings, into the surpassing mystery of his own heart.

As Cardinal Martini suggests, this prayer is the synthesis of Jesus' whole life and the key to understanding him. Like we do each time we pray this prayer at Mass, we began our pilgrimage with confidence, emboldened by Jesus to call God our Father, to request deliverance from evil, to ask for the bread we need, to forgive one another, to do God's will, and to seek always the Kingdom.

Now one thing remains: to say "Amen." Our "Amen" is a commitment to the Christ we have come to know in the prayer he taught us. We move from contemplation to action, from the exploration of feelings to the engagement of the will, from invocation to entrusting oneself, from disciple to apostle. The decisiveness of our "Amen" confirms the first steps we took on our journey and what we learned on the way: "It is though him that we say the 'Amen,' to the glory of God" (2 Corinthians 1:20).